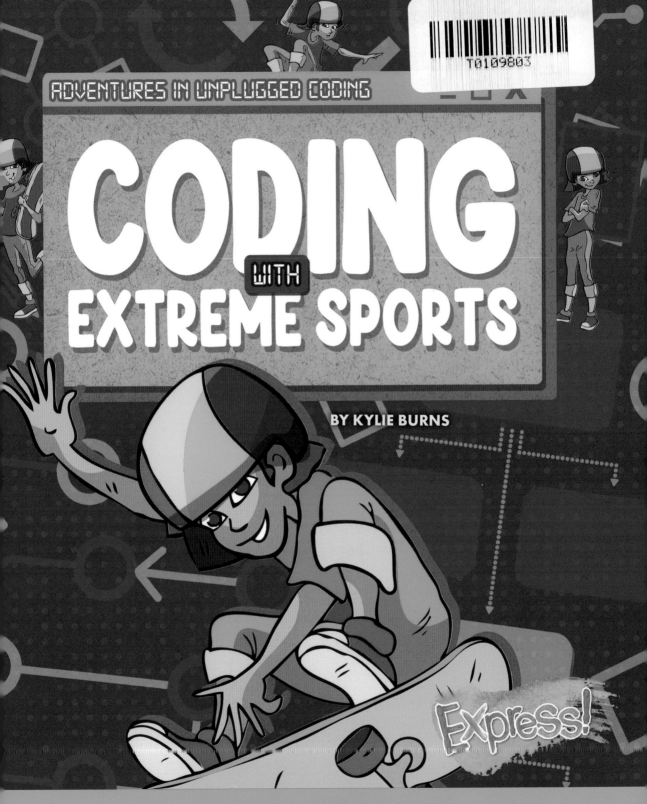

ADVENTURES IN UNPLUGGED CODING

CODING
WITH
EXTREME SPORTS

BY KYLIE BURNS

Express!

BELLWETHER MEDIA • MINNEAPOLIS, MN

Express!

Imagination comes alive in Express! Transform the everyday into the fresh and new, discover ways to stir up flavor and excitement, and experiment with new ideas and materials. Express! makerspace books: where your next creative adventure begins!

This edition first published in 2024 by Bellwether Media, Inc.

No part of this publication may be reproduced in whole or in part without written permission of the publisher. For information regarding permission, write to Bellwether Media, Inc., Attention: Permissions Department, 6012 Blue Circle Drive, Minnetonka, MN 55343.

Library of Congress Cataloging-in-Publication Data

Names: Burns, Kylie, author.
Title: Coding with extreme sports / By Kylie Burns.
Description: Minneapolis, MN : Bellwether Media, Inc., 2024. | Series: Express!: Adventures in unplugged coding | Includes bibliographical references and index. | Audience: Ages 7-13 | Audience: Grades 4-6 | Summary: "Information accompanies instructions for various extreme-sports-themed activities that demonstrate skills needed for coding. The text level and subject matter are intended for students in grades 3 through 8"-- Provided by publisher.
Identifiers: LCCN 2023021291 (print) | LCCN 2023021292 (ebook) | ISBN 9798886875133 (library binding) | ISBN 9798886875638 (paperback) | ISBN 9798886877014 (ebook)
Subjects: LCSH: Extreme sports--Juvenile literature. | Computer programming--Juvenile literature.
Classification: LCC GV749.7 .B87 2024 (print) | LCC GV749.7 (ebook) | DDC 796.04/6--dc23/eng/20230508
LC record available at https://lccn.loc.gov/2023021291
LC ebook record available at https://lccn.loc.gov/2023021292

Text copyright © 2024 by Bellwether Media, Inc. EXPRESS and associated logos are trademarks and/or registered trademarks of Bellwether Media, Inc.

Editors: Sarah Eason and Christina Leaf
Illustrator: Eric Smith
Series Design: Brittany McIntosh
Graphic Designer: Paul Meyerscough

Printed in the United States of America, North Mankato, MN.

TABLE OF CONTENTS _ □ X

Coding is **communicating** with computers so they can perform tasks. If you are given an instruction, the first thing that your brain does is receive the message. Because the instruction is in a language you understand, you can follow the steps to perform the task. It is the same with a computer. **Code** is a language that gives **commands** to a computer.

Programmers, or coders, use code to make programs that tell computers what to do. Programs create actions, just like muscles help athletes perform extreme sports!

Unplugged coding includes activities that use skills such as problem-solving, just like coding with a computer. However, you do not need a computer to do them! The unplugged activities in this book develop skills that will help you become an extreme coder! To make coding even more extreme, in this book we will use extreme sports as our theme!

LET IT RIP!

ROCKY ROAD

In this activity, we will take a look at problem-solving. Solving problems requires looking at something in a different way and coming up with possible solutions.

You are an extreme rock climber! Your task is to climb the face of the mountain and then set up camp near the top. You have a number of things to bring up, but you can only climb carrying one item strapped to your back at a time. How will you get everything safely up the mountain to your campsite? What order will you follow? Write down each step, describing what you would do to solve the problem, and do not leave anything out!

LET'S GET STARTED!

RULES: - - →

1

Carry the following items to the top of the mountain. You can only carry one at a time!
- tent
- sleeping bag
- food
- water jug
- your dog

2

Set up your tent at the top early on, before it gets dark out!

3

Never leave the dog alone with the food because he will eat it!

4

Make sure that the dog has items to protect at all times. If he does, he will stay put. If not, he will run away!

TURN THE PAGE TO SEE HOW YOU DID!

How did you solve the problem? Was it difficult to come up with the steps in your plan? If you tried something that did not work, how did you fix it? Can you think of another solution that might also work? Often there is more than one possible solution to a problem. See below for one way to get all of your gear to the top of the mountain.

Step 1: Take the food up.
Step 2: Climb down and get the tent. Take it up.
Step 3: Get the food and take it back down with you. Leave it there.
Step 4: Take the dog up.
Step 5: Go back down and get the water. Take it up.
Step 6: Go back down and get the sleeping bag. Take it up and place it in the tent.
Step 7: Go back down to get the food and bring it up.

When coders make an error, they do not give up! Instead, they break down the problem into smaller parts. They test out ideas, follow a plan, make mistakes, and think about what they have already done.

CODING CHALLENGE! _ □ X

Try this extreme obstacle course to test your problem-solving skills!

You Will Need:
- 2 or 4 people
- an empty indoor or outdoor space
- 5 to 10 items, such as toys, boxes, or chairs, to place in the space
- blindfolds

If there are two players, one person wears the blindfold. If there are four players, divide into two teams. Each team chooses one player to be blindfolded. The other player or players place the items in a variety of spots so that there is no straight or clear path across the space. The players without blindfolds must instruct their partner about how to get from one end of the space to the other, using only their words to guide them. They may not touch their partner. Teams can take turns, or they can play at the same time. See if you can guide your partner to the finish without bumping into anything!

SNOWBOARD SOLVER

_ □ X

When coders want to program a computer to do a specific task, they begin with what they want the final **outcome** to be. Then, they break it down into specific steps. This is known as **decomposition**.

Try out decomposition in this activity. Your job is to find a way to win a snowboarding race. Use **logic** to come up with the best solution to get through each challenge safely to win the race. There may be risks involved on either path you choose! Think carefully about the steps to reach your goal.

LET'S BREAK IT DOWN!

DID YOU KNOW?

Coders write each individual step or line of code to create an overall instruction the computer understands. The instruction is known as an algorithm.

START

As you race down the hill on your board, you notice two signs. One says "Path A," and the other says "Path B." Most of your competitors take Path A, but one heads off to Path B. Which do you choose?

PATH A

You decide to take Path A and find yourself on a steep slope. You can see a drop-off ahead to your right and a marked path through the thick forest to your left. You choose to:

PATH B

You follow Path B down the slope, but you think you can get the lead by going off the marked course through the trees. You choose to:

Attempt the jump over the drop-off because you think it will win you time. Turn the page and read Outcome 1 to see what happens next.

Take the marked path through the trees. Turn the page and read Outcome 2 to see if you chose wisely!

Take a risk, leaving the racecourse to go through the trees to get ahead. Turn the page and go to Outcome 1.

Stay on the course and count on your extreme skills to speed up. Turn the page and go to Outcome 2.

LET'S SEE HOW YOU DID!

CHECK IT OUT!

How did you do? Find out below!

OUTCOME 1

If you chose the drop-off jump or left the racecourse to go through the trees, oops! You disturbed a grizzly bear! You did not win the competition, and you barely escaped with your life!

OUTCOME 2

If you chose to take the marked path through the trees or stay on the racecourse and make up speed with your awesome skills, congratulations! You raced across the finish line and won the gold medal fair and square!

CODING CHALLENGE! ☐ ✗

Try breaking the following problem into smaller pieces to solve it. You have to make lunch for you and your friend before you hit the slopes again. Your friend suggests peanut butter and jelly sandwiches with no crusts. What do you do first? How many steps will it take? Create your own sandwich-making algorithm, and then test it out in the kitchen!

MOTOCROSS STAR ___ □ X

Coders know that less is more! Having too many instructions can take a long time to write. To get past that problem, coders use **loops**. These are instructions that can be grouped together and repeated within a code.

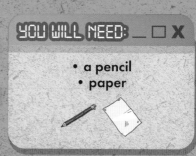

We will look at loops in this activity. Find a way to use loops to get the rider around the motocross course. Can you write the instructions again on a piece of paper, using loops for parts that repeat? Write down your idea using the lowest number of steps. Write "repeat" in front of the step you want to loop. You can include the number of repeats by using "repeat _____ times" to shorten the code.

LET'S GET STARTED!

1. Go straight.
2. Turn right.
3. Do a mid-air trick.
4. Go straight.
5. Turn right.
6. Go straight.
7. Turn right.
8. Pop a wheelie.
9. Go straight.
10. Complete another lap.
11. Complete another lap.
12. Cross the finish line!

FINISH

TURN THE PAGE
TO SEE
HOW YOU DID!

DID YOU KNOW?

When coders loop an instruction in the code, they are telling the computer to repeat an action a number of times, or until a certain event occurs to tell the loop to stop.

Did you find some steps that repeated? Where did you include a loop? Did you test out your steps to see if you won? Below is a loop that shortens the code.

1. Go straight.

2. Turn right.

3. Do a mid-air trick.

4. Repeat 2 times:
   Go straight, turn right.

5. Pop a wheelie.

6. Repeat 2 times:
   Complete another lap.

7. Cross the finish line!

FINISH

HERE'S A TIP!

HERE'S A TIP!

When coders use loops, they sometimes run into errors. If they repeat a loop based on a certain action that never happens, then the loop never ends. This is called an infinite loop. Coders have to think carefully about each instruction, including the instructions for stopping a loop.

CODING CHALLENGE!   _ □ X

You Will Need:
- building blocks such as LEGO bricks
- a toy car or motorcycle
- paper
- a pencil

Create a mini motocross course on a flat surface. Include obstacles and ramps for jumps. Then create a code for your race on paper using at least one loop to shorten your code.

SPORTING CLUES _ □ X

Coders use **variables** as a way of storing information in computer programs. Each variable is named for the kind of information it holds. The variables hold pieces of information called **values**. Values can be different, but they all have the variable in common. For example, if Olympic downhill skiing was a variable, events such as ski jumping, slalom, and freestyle would be values.

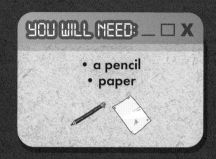
You can learn more about variables and values with this activity. In each box on the next page, the image or images are values of a variable. See if you can find out what the variable is for each box! Keep your eyes peeled!

HERE'S A TIP!

Leaves, grass, and frogs are the values, or information, for what variable? If you guessed the color green, you are right!

LET'S SEE HOW YOU DID!

19

CHECK IT OUT!

Were some variables hard to name for each group of values? Why? How did you name them? The answers for the activity are below. How did your answers match up?

The variable is "orange," and the values are the helmet, paddle, and life jacket.

The variable is "snowboarding," and the values are slopestyle, big air, and halfpipe.

The variable is "extreme sports," and the values are heli-skiing, whitewater rafting, and surfing.

HERE'S A TIP!

There are many things that could represent variables and values in your life. For example, a bowl of cereal is a variable, and the type of cereal is the value. You can change the value by choosing different kinds of cereal, but the variable remains the same. Can you think of other examples?

CODING CHALLENGE!

＿ ☐ **X**

Go on a scavenger hunt in your home or yard. Try to find objects that represent values for these variables:

- something shiny
- something purple
- something with numbers
- something grouped together
- something soft
- something noisy

I HOPE YOU ENJOYED UNPLUGGED CODING!

GLOSSARY

code—instructions for a computer

commands—specific instructions to complete a task

communicating—sharing knowledge or information

decomposition—the process of breaking down a problem or system into smaller parts

logic—thinking that is based on facts or reason

loops—groups of code that can be easily repeated

outcome—a result

values—pieces of information in a code; values are often part of a variable.

variables—parts of a code that store information; variables contain related values.

TO LEARN MORE

☐ X

AT THE LIBRARY

Hutt, Sarah. *Crack the Code!: Activities, Games, and Puzzles That Reveal the World of Coding.* New York, N.Y.: Penguin Workshop, 2018.

McCue, Camille. *Getting Started with Coding: Get Creative with Code!* Indianapolis, Ind.: John Wiley and Sons, 2019.

Prottsman, Kiki. *How to Be a Coder.* New York, N.Y.: DK Publishing, 2019.

ON THE WEB

FACTSURFER

Factsurfer.com gives you a safe, fun way to find more information.

1. Go to www.factsurfer.com.

2. Enter "coding with extreme sports" into the search box and click 🔍.

3. Select your book cover to see a list of related content.

INDEX